Taking Off Emily Dickinson's Clothes

Billy Collins is the author of several books of poetry, including *Nine Horses* and *The Trouble With Poetry and Other Poems*. His poetry has appeared in anthologies, textbooks and a variety of publications in the UK and the US, including *Harper's* and the *New Yorker*. Poet Laureate of the United States for 2001–2003, and currently Poet Laureate of New York State, Collins lives with his wife in northern Westchester County, New York.

Also by Billy Collins

Nine Horses

The Trouble with Poetry
and Other Poems

Billy Collins

Taking Off Emily Dickinson's Clothes

PICADOR

This collection first published 2000 by Picador
an imprint of Pan Macmillan Ltd
20 New Wharf Road, London N1 9RR
Basingstoke and Oxford
Associated companies throughout the world
www.panmacmillan.com

ISBN 978-0-330-37650-1

9

A CIP catalogue record for this book is available from
the British Library.

Typeset by SetSystems Ltd, Saffron Walden, Essex
Printed and bound in the UK by
CPI Mackays, Chatham ME5 8TD

Visit **www.panmacmillan.com** to read more about all our books and to buy
them. You will also find features, author interviews and news of any author
events, and you can sign up for e-newsletters so that you're always first to hear
about our new releases.

Contents

from
Questions About Angels

from
Picnic, Lightning

from

The Apple that
Astonished Paris

Another Reason Why I Don't Keep a Gun in the House

The neighbors' dog will not stop barking.
He is barking the same high, rhythmic bark
that he barks every time they leave the house.
They must switch him on on their way out.

The neighbors' dog will not stop barking.
I close all the windows in the house
and put on a Beethoven symphony full blast
but I can still hear him muffled under the music,
barking, barking, barking,

and now I can see him sitting in the orchestra,
his head raised confidently as if Beethoven
had included a part for barking dog.

When the record finally ends he is still barking,
sitting there in the oboe section barking,
his eyes fixed on the conductor who is
entreating him with his baton

while the other musicians listen in respectful
silence to the famous barking dog solo,
that endless coda that first established
Beethoven as an innovative genius.

Walking Across the Atlantic

I wait for the holiday crowd to clear the beach
before stepping onto the first wave.

Soon I am walking across the Atlantic
thinking about Spain,
checking for whales, waterspouts.

I feel the water holding up my shifting weight.
Tonight I will sleep on its rocking surface.

But for now I try to imagine what
this must look like to the fish below,
the bottoms of my feet appearing, disappearing.

Driving with Animals

I drive this road that whips through woods at night
always searching ahead for the reflective eyes of deer
who will venture onto the grassy verge to browse.

Winter-snug in the warm interior of the car,
I am speeding in the vague nowhere between places,
an arithmetic problem in space and time
which passes slowly on this long solo haul.
I feed cassettes into the dash, light cigarettes,
check the softly lit panel of instruments
measuring motion, pressure, heat, the arcana of the engine,
but there is no red needle to indicate deer.

If I drill my eyes into the night long enough
I will hallucinate shapes in pockets of darkness,
not only deer peering from the fringe of trees,
but other anomalous animals: bison, zebra, even
fish floating in the dreamy pools of fog,

animals released from the mind's deep zoo,
animals we think we see in passing clouds
and in the connected dots of constellations.
Animals parading through the greenery of Eden,
animals on the turning pages of storybooks.
And always deer stepping from the sanctuary of woods,
bolting across the hard ribbon of road in shock,
locked in death-leaps in the sparkle of headlights.

At home as the motor cools in the driveway,
I will feel these rhythms in the quiet of the house.
I will see the heads of deer in the darkened bedroom
and a white flick of tail in the dresser mirror.
I will dream of the sensational touch of a buck's fur
and rock to sleep in the bow and lift of antlers.

Strange Lands

The photographs of the summer trip are spread
across the table now like little mirrors
reflecting our place in European history.

They are the booty of travel, bordered and colorful,
split seconds that we pass to friends after dinner
one by one to make them believe we really found
some sweet elsewhere, away from here.

There we are, the familiar gazing out of the foreign,
stopped in front of a carved Cistercian door,
or leaning obliquely against a kiosk;
frozen behind a blue and white Della Robbia,
or parked at a café table strewn with phrasebooks,
obscured there in the underexposed shadow of an awning.

The waiter in the background, mustache and apron,
is carrying a tray of drinks to others even now
as we flip through the stack another time,
noticing how we tried to be as still as paintings
until the quick rustle of the shutter released us

to walk on again, unfocused, unphotographed,
moving down a street of flowerboxes, motorcycles,
two blurs in the weakening light of evening,
black cameras capped, swaying blindly at our sides.

Hunger

The fox you lug over your shoulder
in a dark sack
has cut a hole with a knife
and escaped.

The sudden lightness makes you think
you are stronger
as you walk back to your small cottage
through a forest that covers the world.

Winter Syntax

A sentence starts out like a lone traveler
heading into a blizzard at midnight,
tilting into the wind, one arm shielding his face,
the tails of his thin coat flapping behind him.

There are easier ways of making sense,
the connoisseurship of gesture, for example.
You hold a girl's face in your hands like a vase.
You lift a gun from the glove compartment
and toss it out the window into the desert heat.
These cool moments are blazing with silence.

The full moon makes sense. When a cloud crosses it
it becomes as eloquent as a bicycle leaning
outside a drugstore or a dog who sleeps all afternoon
in a corner of the couch.

Bare branches in winter are a form of writing.
The unclothed body is autobiography.
Every lake is a vowel, every island a noun.

But the traveler persists in his misery,
struggling all night through the deepening snow,
leaving a faint alphabet of bootprints
on the white hills and the white floors of valleys,
a message for field mice and passing crows.

At dawn he will spot the vine of smoke
rising from your chimney, and when he stands
before you shivering, draped in sparkling frost,
a smile will appear in the beard of icicles,
and the man will express a complete thought.

Plight of the Troubadour

For a good hour I have been singing lays
in langue d'oc to a woman who knows
only langue d'oil, an odd Picard dialect
at that.

The European love lyric is flourishing
with every tremor of my voice,
yet a friend has had to tap my shoulder
to tell me she has not caught a word.

My sentiments are tangled like kites
in the branches of her incomprehension,
and soon I will be lost in an anthology
and poets will no longer wear hats like mine.

Provence will be nothing more
than a pink hue on a map or an answer on a test.
And still the woman smiles over at me
feigning this look of sisterly understanding.

Books

From the heart of this dark, evacuated campus
I can hear the library humming in the night,
a choir of authors murmuring inside their books
along the unlit, alphabetical shelves,
Giovani Pontano next to Pope, Dumas next to his son,
each one stitched into his own private coat,
together forming a low, gigantic chord of language.

I picture a figure in the act of reading,
shoes on a desk, head tilted into the wind of a book,
a man in two worlds, holding the rope of his tie
as the suicide of lovers saturates a page,
or lighting a cigarette in the middle of a theorem.
He moves from paragraph to paragraph
as if touring a house of endless, panelled rooms.

I hear the voice of my mother reading to me
from a chair facing the bed, books about horses and dogs,
and inside her voice lie other distant sounds,
the horrors of a stable ablaze in the night,
a bark that is moving toward the brink of speech.

I watch myself building bookshelves in college,
walls within walls, as rain soaks New England,
or standing in a bookstore in a trench coat.

I see all of us reading ourselves away from ourselves,
straining in circles of light to find more light
until the line of words becomes a trail of crumbs
that we follow across a page of fresh snow.

When evening is shadowing the forest
and small birds flutter down to consume the crumbs,
we have to listen hard to hear the voices
of the boy and his sister receding into the woods.

Death

In the old days news of it traveled by foot.
An aproned woman would wave to her husband
as he receded down the lane, hauling
the stone of the message.

Or someone would bring it out by horse,
a boy galloping, an old man trotting along.
A girl would part a curtain wondering
what anyone would be doing here at this hour,
as he dismounted, hitched the beast to a post,
then lifted the brass knocker, cold as the night.

But today we have the telephone.
You can hear one from where you are right now,
its hammer almost touching the little bell,
ready to summon you, ready to fall from your hand.

Earthling

You have probably come across
those scales in planetariums
that tell you how much you
would weigh on other planets.

You have noticed the fat ones
lingering on the Mars scale
and the emaciated slowing up
the line for Neptune.

As a creature of average weight,
I fail to see the attraction.

Imagine squatting in the wasteland
of Pluto, all five tons of you,
or wandering around Mercury
wondering what to do next with your ounce.

How much better to step onto
the simple bathroom scale,
a happy earthling feeling
the familiar ropes of gravity,

157 pounds standing soaking wet
a respectful distance from the sun.

Child Development

As sure as prehistoric fish grew legs
and sauntered off the beaches into forests
working up some irregular verbs for their
first conversation, so three-year-old children
enter the phase of name-calling.

Every day a new one arrives and is added
to the repertoire. You Dumb Goopyhead,
You Big Sewerface, You Poop-on-the-Floor
(a kind of Navaho ring to that one)
they yell from knee level, their little mugs
flushed with challenge.
Nothing Samuel Johnson would bother tossing out
in a pub, but then the toddlers are not trying
to devastate some fatuous Enlightenment hack.

They are just tormenting their fellow squirts
or going after the attention of the giants
way up there with their cocktails and bad breath
talking baritone nonsense to other giants,
waiting to call them names after thanking
them for the lovely party and hearing the door close.

The mature save their hothead invective
for things: an errant hammer, tire chains,
or receding trains missed by seconds,
though they know in their adult hearts,
even as they threaten to banish Timmy to bed
for his appalling behavior,
that their bosses are Big Fatty Stupids,
their wives are Dopey Dopeheads
and that they themselves are Mr Sillypants.

Putting Down the Cat

The assistant holds her on the table,
the fur hanging limp from her tiny skeleton,
and the veterinarian raises the needle of fluid
which will put the line through her ninth life.

'Painless,' he reassures me, 'like counting
backwards from a hundred,' but I want to tell him
that our poor cat cannot count at all,
much less to a hundred, much less backwards.

Bar Time

In keeping with universal saloon practice,
the clock here is set fifteen minutes ahead
of all the clocks in the outside world.

This makes us a rather advanced group,
doing our drinking in the unknown future,
immune from the cares of the present,
safely harbored a quarter of an hour
beyond the woes of the contemporary scene.

No wonder such thoughtless pleasure derives
from tending the small fire of a cigarette,
from observing this glass of whiskey and ice,
the cold rust I am sipping,

or from having an eye on the street outside
when Ordinary Time slouches past in a topcoat,
rain running off the brim of his hat,
the late edition like a flag in his pocket.

Insomnia

After counting all the sheep in the world
I enumerate the wildebeests, snails,
camels, skylarks, etc.,

then I add up all the zoos and aquariums,
country by country.

By early light I am asleep
in a nightmare about drowning in the Flood,
yelling across the rising water
at preoccupied Noah as his wondrous
ark sails by and begins to grow smaller.

Now a silhouette on the horizon,
the only boat on earth is disappearing.

As I rise and fall on the rocking waves,
I concentrate on the giraffe couple,
their necks craning over the roof,
to keep my life from flashing before me.

After all the animals wink out of sight
I float on my back, eyes closed.
I picture all the fish in creation
leaping a fence in a field of water,
one colorful species after another.

Embrace

You know the parlor trick.
Wrap your arms around your own body
and from the back it looks like
someone is embracing you,
her hands grasping your shirt,
her fingernails teasing your neck.

From the front it is another story.
You never looked so alone,
your crossed elbows and screwy grin.
You could be waiting for a tailor
to fit you for a straitjacket,
one that would hold you really tight.

The Lesson

In the morning when I found History
snoring heavily on the couch,
I took down his overcoat from the rack
and placed its weight over my shoulder blades.

It would protect me on the cold walk
into the village for milk and the paper
and I figured he would not mind,
not after our long conversation the night before.

How unexpected his blustering anger
when I returned covered with icicles,
the way he rummaged through the huge pockets
making sure no major battle or English queen
had fallen out and become lost in the deep snow.

The Rival Poet

The column of your book titles,
always introducing your latest one,
looms over me like Roman architecture.

It is longer than the name
of an Italian countess, longer
than this poem will probably be.

Etched on the head of a pin,
my own production would leave room for
The Lord's Prayer and many dancing angels.
No matter.

In my revenge daydream I am the one
poised on the marble staircase
high above the crowded ballroom.
A retainer in livery announces me
and the Contessa Maria Teresa Isabella
Veronica Multalire Eleganza de Bella Ferrari.

You are the one below
fidgeting in your rented tux
with some local Cindy hanging all over you.

Advice to Writers

Even if it keeps you up all night,
wash down the walls and scrub the floor
of your study before composing a syllable.

Clean the place as if the Pope were on his way.
Spotlessness is the niece of inspiration.

The more you clean, the more brilliant
your writing will be, so do not hesitate to take
to the open fields to scour the undersides
of rocks or swab in the dark forest
upper branches, nests full of eggs.

When you find your way back home
and stow the sponges and brushes under the sink,
you will behold in the light of dawn
the immaculate altar of your desk,
a clean surface in the middle of a clean world.

From a small vase, sparkling blue, lift
a yellow pencil, the sharpest of the bouquet,
and cover pages with tiny sentences
like long rows of devoted ants
that followed you in from the woods.

Schoolsville

Glancing over my shoulder at the past,
I realize the number of students I have taught
is enough to populate a small town.

I can see it nestled in a paper landscape,
chalk dust flurrying down in winter,
nights dark as a blackboard.

The population ages but never graduates.
On hot afternoons they sweat the final in the park
and when it's cold they shiver around stoves
reading disorganized essays out loud.
A bell rings on the hour and everybody zigzags
into the streets with their books.

I forgot all their last names first and their
first names last in alphabetical order.
But the boy who always had his hand up
is an alderman and owns the haberdashery.
The girl who signed her papers in lipstick
leans against the drugstore, smoking,
brushing her hair like a machine.

Their grades are sewn into their clothes
like references to Hawthorne.
The A's stroll along with other A's.
The D's honk whenever they pass another D.

All the creative writing students recline
on the courthouse lawn and play the lute.
Wherever they go, they form a big circle.

Needless to say, I am the mayor.
I live in the white colonial at Maple and Main.
I rarely leave the house. The car deflates
in the driveway. Vines twirl around the porch swing.

Once in a while a student knocks on the door
with a term paper fifteen years late
or a question about Yeats or double-spacing.
And sometimes one will appear in a windowpane
to watch me lecturing the wallpaper,
quizzing the chandelier, reprimanding the air.

The Brooklyn Museum of Art

I will now step over the soft velvet rope
and walk directly into this massive Hudson River
painting and pick my way along the Palisades
with this stick I snapped off a dead tree.

I will skirt the smoky, nestled towns
and seek the path that leads always outward
until I become lost, without a hope
of ever finding the way back to the museum.

I will stand on the bluffs in nineteenth-century clothes,
a dwarf among rock, hills and flowing water,
and I will fish from the banks in a straw hat
which will feel like a brush stroke on my head.

And I will hide in the green covers of forests
so no appreciator of Frederick Edwin Church,
leaning over the soft velvet rope,
will spot my tiny figure moving in the stillness
and cry out, pointing for the others to see,

and be thought mad and led away to a cell
where there is no vaulting landscape to explore,
none of this bird song that halts me in my tracks,
and no wide curving of this river that draws
my steps toward the misty vanishing point.

from

Questions About Angels

American Sonnet

We do not speak like Petrarch or wear a hat like Spenser
and it is not fourteen lines
like furrows in a small, carefully plowed field

but the picture postcard, a poem on vacation,
that forces us to sing our songs in little rooms
or pour our sentiments into measuring cups.

We write on the back of a waterfall or lake,
adding to the view a caption as conventional
as an Elizabethan woman's heliocentric eyes.

We locate an adjective for the weather.
We announce that we are having a wonderful time.
We express the wish that you were here

and hide the wish that we were where you are,
walking back from the mailbox, your head lowered
as you read and turn the thin message in your hands.

A slice of this place, a length of white beach,
a piazza or carved spires of a cathedral
will pierce the familiar place where you remain,

and you will toss on the table this reversible display:
a few square inches of where we have strayed
and a compression of what we feel.

A History of Weather

It is the kind of spring morning – candid sunlight
elucidating the air, a flower-ruffling breeze –
that makes me want to begin a history of weather,
a ten-volume elegy for the atmospheres of the past,
the envelopes that have moved around the moving globe.

It will open by examining the cirrus clouds
that are now sweeping over this house into the next state,
and every chapter will step backwards in time
to illustrate the rain that fell on battlefields
and the winds that attended beheadings, coronations.

The snow flurries of Victorian London will be surveyed
along with the gales that blew off Renaissance caps.
The tornadoes of the Middle Ages will be explicated
and the long, overcast days of the Dark Ages.
There will be a section on the frozen nights of antiquity
and on the heat that shimmered in the deserts of the Bible.

The study will be hailed as ambitious and definitive,
for it will cover even the climate before the Flood
when showers moistened Eden and will conclude
with the mysteries of the weather before history
when unseen clouds drifted over an unpeopled world,
when not a soul lay in any of earth's meadows gazing up
at the passing of enormous faces and animal shapes,
his jacket bunched into a pillow, an open book on his chest.

Student of Clouds

The emotion is to be found in the clouds,
not in the green solids of the sloping hills
or even in the gray signatures of rivers,
according to Constable, who was a student of clouds
and filled shelves of sketchbooks with their motion,
their lofty gesturing and sudden implication of weather.

Outdoors, he must have looked up thousands of times,
his pencil trying to keep pace with their high voyaging
and the silent commotion of their eddying and flow.
Clouds would move beyond the outlines he would draw
as they moved within themselves, tumbling into their centers
and swirling off at the burning edges in vapors
to dissipate into the universal blue of the sky.

In photographs we can stop all this movement now
long enough to tag them with their Latin names.
Cirrus, nimbus, stratocumulus –
dizzying, romantic, authoritarian –
they bear their titles over the schoolhouses below
where their shapes and meanings are memorized.

High on the soft blue canvases of Constable
they are stuck in pigment but his clouds appear
to be moving still in the wind of his brush,
inching out of England and the nineteenth century
and sailing over these meadows where I am walking,
bareheaded beneath this cupola of motion,
my thoughts arranged like paint on a high blue ceiling.

Candle Hat

In most self-portraits it is the face that dominates:
Cézanne is a pair of eyes swimming in brushstrokes,
Van Gogh stares out of a halo of swirling darkness,
Rembrandt looks relieved as if he were taking a breather
from painting *The Blinding of Samson*.

But in this one Goya stands well back from the mirror
and is seen posed in the clutter of his studio
addressing a canvas tilted back on a tall easel.

He appears to be smiling out at us as if he knew
we would be amused by the extraordinary hat on his head
which is fitted around the brim with candle holders,
a device that allowed him to work into the night.

You can only wonder what it would be like
to be wearing such a chandelier on your head
as if you were a walking dining room or concert hall.

But once you see this hat there is no need to read
any biography of Goya or to memorize his dates.

To understand Goya you only have to imagine him
lighting the candles one by one, then placing
the hat on his head, ready for a night of work.

Imagine him surprising his wife with his new invention,
then laughing like a birthday cake when she saw the glow.

Imagine him flickering through the rooms of his house
with all the shadows flying across the walls.

Imagine a lost traveler knocking on his door
one dark night in the hill country of Spain.
'Come in,' he would say, 'I was just painting myself,'
as he stood in the doorway holding up the wand of a brush,
illuminated in the blaze of his famous candle hat.

Forgetfulness

The name of the author is the first to go
followed obediently by the title, the plot,
the heartbreaking conclusion, the entire novel
which suddenly becomes one you have never read, never
    even heard of.

It is as if, one by one, the memories you used to harbor
decided to retire to the southern hemisphere of the brain,
to a little fishing village where there are no phones.

Long ago you kissed the names of the nine Muses goodbye
and watched the quadratic equation pack its bag,
and even now as you memorize the order of the planets,

something else is slipping away, a state flower perhaps,
the address of an uncle, the capital of Paraguay.

Whatever it is you are struggling to remember
it is not poised on the tip of your tongue,
not even lurking in some obscure corner of your spleen.

It has floated away down a dark mythological river
whose name begins with an *L* as far as you can recall,
well on your own way to oblivion where you will join those
who have even forgotten how to swim and how to ride a
    bicycle.

No wonder you rise in the middle of the night
to look up the date of a famous battle in a book on war.
No wonder the moon in the window seems to have drifted
out of a love poem that you used to know by heart.

The Death of Allegory

I am wondering what became of all those tall abstractions
that used to pose, robed and statuesque, in paintings
and parade about on the pages of the Renaissance
displaying their capital letters like license plates.

Truth cantering on a powerful horse,
Chastity, eyes downcast, fluttering with veils.
Each one was marble come to life, a thought in a coat,
Courtesy bowing with one hand always extended,

Villainy sharpening an instrument behind a wall,
Reason with her crown and Constancy alert behind a helm.
They are all retired now, consigned to a Florida for tropes.
Justice is there standing by an open refrigerator.

Valor lies in bed listening to the rain.
Even Death has nothing to do but mend his cloak and hood,
and all their props are locked away in a warehouse,
hourglasses, globes, blindfolds and shackles.

Even if you called them back, there are no places left
for them to go, no Garden of Mirth or Bower of Bliss.
The Valley of Forgiveness is lined with condominiums
and chain saws are howling in the Forest of Despair.

Here on the table near the window is a vase of peonies
and next to it black binoculars and a money clip,
exactly the kind of thing we now prefer,
objects that sit quietly on a line in lower case,

themselves and nothing more, a wheelbarrow,
an empty mailbox, a razor blade resting in a glass ashtray.
As for the others, the great ideas on horseback
and the long-haired virtues in embroidered gowns,

it looks as though they have traveled down
that road you see on the final page of storybooks,
the one that winds up a green hillside and disappears
into an unseen valley where everyone must be fast asleep.

Questions About Angels

Of all the questions you might want to ask
about angels, the only one you ever hear
is how many can dance on the head of a pin.

No curiosity about how they pass the eternal time
besides circling the Throne chanting in Latin
or delivering a crust of bread to a hermit on earth
or guiding a boy and girl across a rickety wooden bridge.

Do they fly through God's body and come out singing?
Do they swing like children from the hinges
of the spirit world saying their names backwards and
    forwards?
Do they sit alone in little gardens changing colors?

What about their sleeping habits, the fabric of their robes,
their diet of unfiltered divine light?
What goes on inside their luminous heads? Is there a wall
these tall presences can look over and see hell?

If an angel fell off a cloud would he leave a hole
in a river and would the hole float along endlessly
filled with the silent letters of every angelic word?

If an angel delivered the mail would he arrive
in a blinding rush of wings or would he just assume
the appearance of the regular mailman and
whistle up the driveway reading the postcards?

No, the medieval theologians control the court.
The only question you ever hear is about
the little dance floor on the head of a pin
where halos are meant to converge and drift invisibly.

It is designed to make us think in millions,
billions, to make us run out of numbers and collapse
into infinity, but perhaps the answer is simply one:
one female angel dancing alone in her stocking feet,
a small jazz combo working in the background.

She sways like a branch in the wind, her beautiful
eyes closed, and the tall thin bassist leans over
to glance at his watch because she has been dancing
forever, and now it is very late, even for musicians.

The Dead

The dead are always looking down on us, they say,
while we are putting on our shoes or making a sandwich,
they are looking down through the glass-bottom boats of
    heaven
as they row themselves slowly through eternity.

They watch the tops of our heads moving below on earth,
and when we lie down in a field or on a couch,
drugged perhaps by the hum of a warm afternoon,
they think we are looking back at them,

which makes them lift their oars and fall silent
and wait, like parents, for us to close our eyes.

Purity

My favorite time to write is in the late afternoon,
weekdays, particularly Wednesdays.
This is how I go about it:
I take a fresh pot of tea into my study and close the door.
Then I remove my clothes and leave them in a pile
as if I had melted to death and my legacy consisted of only
a white shirt, a pair of pants and a pot of cold tea.

Then I remove my flesh and hang it over a chair.
I slide it off my bones like a silken garment.
I do this so that what I write will be pure,
completely rinsed of the carnal,
uncontaminated by the preoccupations of the body.

Finally I remove each of my organs and arrange them
on a small table near the window.
I do not want to hear their ancient rhythms
when I am trying to tap out my own drumbeat.

Now I sit down at the desk, ready to begin.
I am entirely pure: nothing but a skeleton at a typewriter.

I should mention that sometimes I leave my penis on.
I find it difficult to ignore the temptation.
Then I am a skeleton with a penis at a typewriter.

In this condition I write extraordinary love poems,
most of them exploiting the connection between sex and death.

I am concentration itself: I exist in a universe
where there is nothing but sex, death, and typewriting.

After a spell of this I remove my penis too.
Then I am all skull and bones typing into the afternoon.
Just the absolute essentials, no flounces.
Now I write only about death, most classical of themes
in language light as the air between my ribs.

Afterward, I reward myself by going for a drive at sunset.
I replace my organs and slip back into my flesh
and clothes. Then I back the car out of the garage
and speed through woods on winding country roads,
passing stone walls, farmhouses, and frozen ponds,
all perfectly arranged like words in a famous sonnet.

Wolf

A wolf is reading a book of fairy tales.
The moon hangs over the forest, a lamp.

He is not assuming a human position,
say, cross-legged against a tree,
as he would in a cartoon.

This is a real wolf, standing on all fours,
his rich fur bristling in the night air,
his head bent over the book open on the ground.

He does not sit down, for the words
would be too far away to be legible,
and it is with difficulty that he turns
each page with his nose and forepaws.

When he finishes the last tale
he lies down in pine needles.
He thinks about what he has read,
the stories passing over his mind
like the clouds crossing the moon.

A zigzag of wind shakes down hazelnuts.
The eyes of owls yellow in the branches.

The wolf now paces restlessly in circles
around the book until he is absorbed
by the power of its narration,
making him one of its illustrations,
a small paper wolf, flat as print.

Later that night, lost in a town of pigs,
he knocks over houses with his breath.

The Man in the Moon

He used to frighten me in the nights of childhood,
the wide adult face, enormous, stern, aloft.
I could not imagine such loneliness, such coldness.

But tonight as I drive home over these hilly roads
I see him sinking behind stands of winter trees
and rising again to show his familiar face.

And when he comes into full view over open fields
he looks like a young man who has fallen in love
with the dark earth,

a pale bachelor, well-groomed and full of melancholy,
his round mouth open
as if he had just broken into song.

Memento Mori

There is no need for me to keep a skull on my desk,
to stand with one foot up on the ruins of Rome,
or wear a locket with the sliver of a saint's bone.

It is enough to realize that every common object
in this sunny little room will outlive me –
the carpet, radio, bookstand and rocker.

Not one of these things will attend my burial,
not even this dented goosenecked lamp
with its steady benediction of light,

though I could put worse things in my mind
than the image of it waddling across the cemetery
like an old servant, dragging the tail of its cord,
the small circle of mourners parting to make room.

The Wires of the Night

I thought about his death for so many hours,
tangled there in the wires of the night,
that it came to have a body and dimensions,
more than a voice shaking over the telephone
or the black obituary boldface of name and dates.

His death now had an entrance and an exit, doors and stairs,
windows and shutters, which are the motionless wings
of windows. His death had a head and clothes,
the white shirt and baggy trousers of death.

His death had pages, a dark leather cover, an index,
and the print was too minuscule for anyone to read.
His death had hinges and bolts which were oiled and locked,
had a loud motor, four tires, an antenna which listened
to the wind, and a mirror in which you could see the past.

His death had sockets and keys, it had walls and beams.
It had a handle which you could not hold and a floor
you could not lie down on in the middle of the night.

In the freakish pink and grey of dawn I took
his death to bed with me and his death was my bed
and in every corner of the room it hid from the light,

and then it was the light of day and the next day
and all the days to follow, and it moved into the future
like the sharp tip of a pen moving across an empty page.

Vade Mecum

I want the scissors to be sharp
and the table to be perfectly level
when you cut me out of my life
and paste me in that book you always carry.

Night Sand

When you injure me, as you must one day,
I will move off like the slow armadillo over night sand,
ambulating secretly inside his armor,

ready to burrow deep or curl himself into a ball
which will shelter his soft head, soft feet
and tail from the heavy, rhythmic blows.

Now can you see the silhouettes of ranchers' hats
and sticks raised against the pink desert sky?

Not Touching

The valentine of desire is pasted over my heart
and still we are not touching, like things

in a poorly done still life
where the knife appears to be floating over the plate
which is itself hovering above the table somehow,

the entire arrangement of apple, pear and wineglass
having forgotten the law of gravity,
refusing to be still,

as if the painter had caught them all
in a rare moment of slow flight
just before they drifted out of the room
through a window of perfectly realistic sunlight.

Invective

Turn away from me, you, and get lost in the past.
Back to ancient Rome you go, with its parallel columns and
  syllogisms.
Stuff yourself with berries, eat lying on your side.
Suck balls of snow carried down from the Alps for dessert.

I don't care. I am leaving too, but for the margins of history,
to a western corner of ninth century Ireland I go,
to a vanishing, grey country far beyond your call.

There I will dwell with badgers, fish and deer,
birds piercing the air and the sound of little bells.
I will stand in pastures of watercress by the salmon-lashing sea.
I will stare into the cold, unblinking eyes of cows.

The History Teacher

Trying to protect his students' innocence
he told them the Ice Age was really just
the Chilly Age, a period of a million years
when everyone had to wear sweaters.

And the Stone Age became the Gravel Age,
named after the long driveways of the time.

The Spanish Inquisition was nothing more
than an outbreak of questions such as
'How far is it from here to Madrid?'
'What do you call the matador's hat?'

The War of the Roses took place in a garden,
and the Enola Gay dropped one tiny atom
on Japan.

The children would leave his classroom
for the playground to torment the weak
and the smart,
mussing up their hair and breaking their glasses,

while he gathered up his notes and walked home
past flower beds and white picket fences,
wondering if they would believe that soldiers
in the Boer War told long, rambling stories
designed to make the enemy nod off.

Nostalgia

Remember the 1340s? We were doing a dance called the
    Catapult.
You always wore brown, the color craze of the decade,
and I was draped in one of those capes that were popular,
the ones with unicorns and pomegranates in needlework.
Everyone would pause for beer and onions in the afternoon,
and at night we would play a game called 'Find the Cow.'
Everything was hand-lettered then, not like today.

Where has the summer of 1572 gone? Brocade and sonnet
marathons were the rage. We used to dress up in the flags
of rival baronies and conquer one another in cold rooms of
    stone.
Out on the dance floor we were all doing the Struggle
while your sister practiced the Daphne all alone in her room.
We borrowed the jargon of farriers for our slang.
These days language seems transparent, a badly broken code.

The 1790s will never come again. Childhood was big.
People would take walks to the very tops of hills
and write down what they saw in their journals without
    speaking.
Our collars were high and our hats were extremely soft.
We would surprise each other with alphabets made of twigs.
It was a wonderful time to be alive, or even dead.

I am very fond of the period between 1815 and 1821.
Europe trembled while we sat still for our portraits.
And I would love to return to 1901 if only for a moment,
time enough to wind up a music box and do a few dance steps,
or shoot me back to 1922 or 1941, or at least let me
recapture the serenity of last month when we picked
berries and glided through afternoons in a canoe.

Even this morning would be an improvement over the present.
I was in the garden then, surrounded by the hum of bees
and the Latin names of flowers, watching the early light
flash off the slanted windows of the greenhouse
and silver the limbs on the rows of dark hemlocks.

As usual, I was thinking about the moments of the past,
letting my memory rush over them like water
rushing over the stones on the bottom of a stream.
I was even thinking a little about the future, that place
where people are doing a dance we cannot imagine,
a dance whose name we can only guess.

from

The Art of Drowning

Consolation

How agreeable it is not to be touring Italy this summer,
wandering her cities and ascending her torrid hilltowns.
How much better to cruise these local, familiar streets,
fully grasping the meaning of every roadsign and billboard
and all the sudden hand gestures of my compatriots.

There are no abbeys here, no crumbling frescoes or famous
domes and there is no need to memorize a succession
of kings or tour the dripping corners of a dungeon.
No need to stand around a sarcophagus, see Napoleon's
little bed on Elba, or view the bones of a saint under glass.

How much better to command the simple precinct of home
than be dwarfed by pillar, arch, and basilica.
Why hide my head in phrase books and wrinkled maps?
Why feed scenery into a hungry, one-eyed camera
eager to eat the world one monument at a time?

Instead of slouching in a café ignorant of the word for ice,
I will head down to the coffee shop and the waitress
known as Dot. I will slide into the flow of the morning
paper, all language barriers down,
rivers of idiom running freely, eggs over easy on the way.

And after breakfast, I will not have to find someone
willing to photograph me with my arm around the owner.
I will not puzzle over the bill or record in a journal
what I had to eat and how the sun came in the window.
It is enough to climb back into the car

as if it were the great car of English itself
and sounding my loud vernacular horn, speed off
down a road that will never lead to Rome, nor even Bologna.

Osso Buco

I love the sound of the bone against the plate
and the fortress-like look of it
lying before me in a moat of risotto,
the meat soft as the leg of an angel
who has lived a purely airborne existence.
And best of all, the secret marrow,
the invaded privacy of the animal
prized out with a knife and swallowed down
with cold, exhilarating wine.

I am swaying now in the hour after dinner.
a citizen tilted back on his chair,
a creature with a full stomach –
something you don't hear much about in poetry,
that sanctuary of hunger and deprivation.
You know: the driving rain, the boots by the door,
small birds searching for berries in winter.

But tonight, the lion of contentment
has placed a warm, heavy paw on my chest,
and I can only close my eyes and listen
to the drums of woe throbbing in the distance
and the sound of my wife's laughter
on the telephone in the next room,
the woman who cooked the savory osso buco,
who pointed to show the butcher the ones she wanted.
She who talks to her faraway friend
while I linger here at the table
with a hot, companionable cup of tea,
feeling like one of the friendly natives,
a reliable guide, maybe even the chief's favorite son.

Somewhere, a man is crawling up a rocky hillside
on bleeding knees and palms, an Irish penitent
carrying the stone of the world in his stomach;
and elsewhere people of all nations stare
at one another across a long, empty table.

But here, the candles give off their warm glow,
the same light that Shakespeare and Izaac Walton wrote by,
the light that lit and shadowed the faces of history.
Only now it plays on the blue plates,
the crumpled napkins, the crossed knife and fork.

In a while, one of us will go up to bed
and the other one will follow.
Then we will slip below the surface of the night
into miles of water, drifting down and down
to the dark, soundless bottom
until the weight of dreams pulls us lower still,
below the shale and layered rock,
beneath the strata of hunger and pleasure,
into the broken bones of the earth itself,
into the marrow of the only place we know.

Directions

You know the brick path in back of the house,
the one you see from the kitchen window,
the one that bends around the far end of the garden
where all the yellow primroses are?
And you know how if you leave the path
and walk up into the woods you come
to a heap of rocks, probably pushed
down during the horrors of the Ice Age,
and a grove of tall hemlocks, dark green now
against the light brown fallen leaves?
And farther on, you know
the small footbridge with the broken railing
and if you go beyond that you arrive
at the bottom of that sheep's head hill?
Well, if you start climbing, and you
might have to grab hold of a sapling
when the going gets steep,
you will eventually come to a long stone
ridge with a border of pine trees
which is as high as you can go
and a good enough place to stop.

The best time is late afternoon
when the sun strobes through
the columns of trees as you are hiking up,
and when you find an agreeable rock
to sit on, you will be able to see
the light pouring down into the woods
and breaking into the shapes and tones
of things and you will hear nothing
but a sprig of birdsong or the leafy
falling of a cone or nut through the trees,
and if this is your day you might even
spot a hare or feel the wing-beats of geese
driving overhead toward some destination.

But it is hard to speak of these things
how the voices of light enter the body
and begin to recite their stories
how the earth holds us painfully against
its breast made of humus and brambles
how we who will soon be gone regard
the entities that continue to return
greener than ever, spring water flowing
through a meadow and the shadows of clouds
passing over the hills and the ground
where we stand in the tremble of thought
taking the vast outside into ourselves.

Still, let me know before you set out.
Come knock on my door
and I will walk with you as far as the garden
with one hand on your shoulder.
I will even watch after you and not turn back
to the house until you disappear
into the crowd of maple and ash,
heading up toward the hill,
piercing the ground with your stick.

Sunday Morning with
the Sensational Nightingales

It was not the Five Mississippi Blind Boys
who lifted me off the ground
that Sunday morning
as I drove down for the paper, some oranges, and bread.
Nor was it the Dixie Hummingbirds
or the Soul Stirrers, despite their quickening name,
or even the Swan Silvertones
who inspired me to look over the commotion of trees
into the open vault of the sky.

No, it was the Sensational Nightingales
who happened to be singing on the gospel
station early that Sunday morning
and must be credited with the bumping up
of my spirit, the arousal of the mice within.

I have always loved this harmony,
like four, sometimes five trains running
side by side over a contoured landscape –
make that a shimmering, red-dirt landscape,
wildflowers growing along the silver tracks,
lace tablecloths covering the hills,
the men and women in white shirts and dresses
walking in the direction of a tall steeple.
Sunday morning in a perfect Georgia.

But I am not here to describe the sound
of the falsetto whine, sepulchral bass,
alto and tenor fitted snugly in between;
only to witness my own minor ascension
that morning as they sang, so parallel,
about the usual themes,
the garden of suffering,
the beads of blood on the forehead,
the stone before the hillside tomb,
and the ancient rolling waters
we would all have to cross some day.

God bless the Sensational Nightingales,
I thought as I turned up the volume,
God bless their families and their powder blue suits.
They are a far cry from the quiet kneeling
I was raised with,
a far, hand-clapping cry from the candles
that glowed in the alcoves
and the fixed eyes of saints staring down
from their corners.

Oh, my cap was on straight that Sunday morning
and I was fine keeping the car on the road.
No one would ever have guessed
I was being lifted into the air by nightingales,
hoisted by their beaks like a long banner
that curls across an empty blue sky,
caught up in the annunciation
of these high, most encouraging tidings.

The Best Cigarette

There are many that I miss,
having sent my last one out a car window
sparking along the road one night, years ago.

The heralded ones, of course:
after sex, the two glowing tips
now the lights of a single ship;
at the end of a long dinner
with more wine to come
and a smoke ring coasting into the chandelier;
or on a white beach,
holding one with fingers still wet from a swim.

How bittersweet these punctuations
of flame and gesture;
but the best were on those mornings
when I would have a little something going
in the typewriter,
the sun bright in the windows,
maybe some Berlioz on in the background.
I would go into the kitchen for coffee
and on the way back to the page,
curled in its roller,
I would light one up and feel
its dry rush mix with the dark taste of coffee.

Then I would be my own locomotive,
trailing behind me as I returned to work
little puffs of smoke,
indicators of progress,
signs of industry and thought,
the signal that told the nineteenth century
it was moving forward.
That was the best cigarette,
when I would steam into the study
full of vaporous hope
and stand there,
the big headlamp of my face
pointed down at all the words in parallel lines.

Days

Each one *is* a gift, no doubt,
mysteriously placed in your waking hand
or set upon your forehead
moments before you open your eyes.

Today begins cold and bright,
the ground heavy with snow
and the thick masonry of ice,
the sun glinting off the turrets of clouds.

Through the calm eye of the window
everything is in its place
but so precariously
this day might be resting somehow

on the one before it,
all the days of the past stacked high
like the impossible tower of dishes
entertainers used to build on stage.

No wonder you find yourself
perched on the top of a tall ladder
hoping to add one more.
Just another Wednesday

you whisper,
then holding your breath,
place this cup on yesterday's saucer
without the slightest clink.

Tuesday, June 4, 1991

By the time I get myself out of bed, my wife has left
the house to take her botany final and the painter
has arrived in his van and is already painting
the columns of the front porch white and the decking gray.

It is early June, a breezy and sun-riddled Tuesday
that would quickly be forgotten were it not for my
writing these few things down as I sit here empty-headed
at the typewriter with a cup of coffee, light and sweet.

I feel like the secretary to the morning whose only
responsibility is to take down its bright, airy dictation
until it's time to go to lunch with the other girls,
all of us ordering the cottage cheese with half a pear.

This is what stenographers do in courtrooms, too,
alert at their miniature machines taking down every word.
When there is a silence they sit still as I do, waiting
and listening, fingers resting lightly on the keys.

This is also what Samuel Pepys did, jotting down in
private ciphers minor events that would have otherwise
slipped into the dark amnesiac waters of the Thames.
His vigilance finally paid off when London caught fire

as mine does when the painter comes in for coffee
and says how much he likes this slow vocal rendition
of 'You Don't Know What Love Is' and I figure I will
make him a tape when he goes back to his brushes and pails.

Under the music I can hear the rush of cars and trucks
on the highway and every so often the new kitten, Felix,
hops into my lap and watches my fingers drumming out
a running record of this particular June Tuesday

as it unrolls before my eyes, a long intricate carpet
that I am walking on slowly with my head bowed
knowing that it is leading me to the quiet shrine
of the afternoon and the melancholy candles of evening.

If I look up, I see out the window the white stars
of clematis climbing a ladder of strings, a woodpile,
a stack of faded bricks, a small green garden of herbs,
things you would expect to find outside a window,

all written down now and placed in the setting
of a stanza as unalterably as they are seated
in their chairs in the ontological rooms of the world.
Yes, this is the kind of job I could succeed in,

an unpaid but contented amanuensis whose hands
are two birds fluttering on the lettered keys,
whose eyes see sunlight splashing through the leaves,
and the bright pink asterisks of honeysuckle

and the piano at the other end of this room with
its small vase of faded flowers and its empty bench.
So convinced am I that I have found my vocation,
tomorrow I will begin my chronicling earlier, at dawn,

a time when hangmen and farmers are up and doing,
when men holding pistols stand in a field back to back.
It is the time the ancients imagined in robes, as Eos
or Aurora, who would leave her sleeping husband in bed,

not to take her botany final, but to pull the sun,
her brother, over the horizon's brilliant rim,
her four-horse chariot aimed at the zenith of the sky.
But tomorrow, dawn will come the way I picture her,

barefoot and disheveled, standing outside my window
in one of the fragile cotton dresses of the poor.
She will look in at me with her thin arms extended,
offering a handful of birdsong and a small cup of light.

Canada

I am writing this on a strip of white birch bark
that I cut from a tree with a pen knife.
There is no other way to express adequately
the immensity of the clouds that are passing over the farms
and wooded lakes of Ontario and the endless visibility
that hands you the horizon on a platter.

I am also writing this in a wooden canoe,
a point of balance in the middle of Lake Couchiching,
resting the birch bark against my knees.
I can feel the sun's hands on my bare back,
but I am thinking of winter,
snow piled up in all the provinces
and the solemnity of the long grain ships
that pass the cold months moored at Owen Sound.

O Canada, as the anthem goes,
scene of my boyhood summers,
you are the pack of Sweet Caporals on the table,
you are the dove-soft train whistle in the night,
you are the empty chair at the end of an empty dock.
You are the shelves of books in a lakeside cottage:
Gift from the Sea by Anne Morrow Lindbergh,
A Child's Garden of Verses by Robert Louis Stevenson,
Ann of Avonlea by L. M. Montgomery,
So You're Going to Paris! by Clara E. Laughlin,
and *Peril Over the Airport*, one
of the Vicky Barr Flight Stewardess series
by Helen Wills whom some will remember
as the author of the Cherry Ames Nurse stories.

What has become of the languorous girls
who would pass the long limp summer evenings reading
Cherry Ames, Student Nurse, Cherry Ames, Senior Nurse,
Cherry Ames, Chief Nurse, and *Cherry Ames, Flight Nurse*?
Where are they now, the ones who shared her adventures
as a veterans' nurse, private duty nurse, visiting nurse,
cruise nurse, night supervisor, mountaineer nurse,
dude ranch nurse (there is little she has not done),
rest home nurse, department store nurse,
boarding school nurse, and country doctor's nurse?

O Canada, I have not forgotten you,
and as I kneel in my canoe, beholding this vision
of a bookcase, I pray that I remain in your vast,
polar, North American memory.
You are the paddle, the snowshoe, the cabin in the pines.
You are Jean de Brébeuf with his martyr's necklace of hatchet
      heads.
You are the moose in the clearing and the moosehead on the
      wall.
You are the rapids, the propeller, the kerosene lamp.
You are the dust that coats the roadside berries.
But not only that.
You are the two boys with pails walking along that road,
and one of them, the taller one minus the straw hat, is me.

Death Beds

The ancients were talkative on theirs,
so many agencies needed to be addressed:
the gods of departure who controlled
the seven portals of the world,
the ferrymen leaning on their smooth oars,
the eternal pilots, immortal conductors,
and that was just the transportation.

Japanese monks would motion for a tablet,
sometimes, an inkwell and a brush
so they could leave behind the dark,
wet strokes of a short poem –
a drop of rain on a yellow leaf.
One described the night clouds
and the moon making its million-mile journey.

Medieval Christians who could read
could read a treatise on the subject:
De Arte Moriendi, On the Art of Dying,
pages of instruction on what to do in bed,
how to set the heart right,
how to point the soul upward
and listen to the prayer of one's own breathing.

Some pale Victorians in their tubercular
throes would ask for a looking glass
so they could behold the seraphic glow
the dry fever brought to their faces.
A few even had a photographer summoned
to open his tripod in the sickroom
and disappear under the heavy black cloth
as the subject, more or less, was doing the same.

Then there were the wits,
using their last breath to exhale a line,
a devastating capper, as if the world
were simply a large gallery buzzing with people,
and now it was time to throw on a long scarf
and make an exit, leaving
it to someone else to close the door.

Some lie on their backs for months,
students of the ceiling,
others roll over once and are gone.
Some bellow for a priest
and make the one confession no one doubts.
And you, and I, too, may lie on ours,
the vigilant family in a semicircle,
or the night nurse holding our hand
in the dark, or alone.
There will be no ink, mirror, or Latin book,
though the wallpaper may be tasteless
and you may feel yourself entering a myth.

I would hope for a window,
the usual frame of reference,
a clear sky, or thin high clouds,
an abundance of sun, a cool pillow.
And I would expect just at the end
a moment of pure awareness
when I could feel the solitary pea under the mattress
and pick out the dot of a hawk lost in the blue.

On Turning Ten

The whole idea of it makes me feel
like I'm coming down with something,
something worse than any stomach ache
or the headaches I get from reading in bad light –
a kind of measles of the spirit,
a mumps of the psyche,
a disfiguring chicken pox of the soul.

You tell me it is too early to be looking back,
but that is because you have forgotten
the perfect simplicity of being one
and the beautiful complexity introduced by two.
But I can lie on my bed and remember every digit.
At four I was an Arabian wizard.
I could make myself invisible
by drinking a glass of milk a certain way.
At seven I was a soldier, at nine a prince.

But now I am mostly at the window
watching the late afternoon light.
Back then it never fell so solemnly
against the side of my tree house,
and my bicycle never leaned against the garage
as it does today,
all the dark blue speed drained out of it.

This is the beginning of sadness, I say to myself,
as I walk through the universe in my sneakers.
It is time to say good-bye to my imaginary friends,
time to turn the first big number.

It seems only yesterday I used to believe
there was nothing under my skin but light.
If you cut me I would shine.
But now when I fall upon the sidewalks of life,
I skin my knees. I bleed.

Workshop

I might as well begin by saying how much I like the title.
It gets me right away because I'm in a workshop now
so immediately the poem has my attention,
like the ancient mariner grabbing me by the sleeve.

And I like the first couple of stanzas,
the way they establish this mode of self-pointing
that runs through the whole poem
and tells us that words are food thrown down
on the ground for other words to eat.
I can almost taste the tail of the snake
in its own mouth,
if you know what I mean.

But what I'm not sure about is the voice
which sounds in places very casual, very blue jeans,
but other times seems standoffish,
professorial in the worst sense of the word
like the poem is blowing pipe smoke in my face.
But maybe that's just what it wants to do.

What I did find engaging were the middle stanzas,
especially the fourth one.
I like the image of clouds flying like lozenges
which gives me a very clear picture.
And I really like how this drawbridge operator
just appears out of the blue
with his feet up on the iron railing
and his fishing pole jigging – I like jigging –
a hook in the slow industrial canal below.
I love slow industrial canal below. All those *l*'s.

Maybe it's just me,
but the next stanza is where I start to have a problem.
I mean how can the evening bump into the stars?
And what's an obbligato of snow?
Also, I roam the decaffeinated streets.
At that point I'm lost. I need help.

The other thing that throws me off,
and maybe this is just me,
is the way the scene keeps shifting around.
First, we're in this big aerodrome
and the speaker is inspecting a row of dirigibles,
which makes me think this could be a dream.
Then he takes us into his garden,
the part with the dahlias and the coiling hose,
though that's nice, the coiling hose,
but then I'm not sure where we're supposed to be.
The rain and the mint green light,
that makes it feel outdoors, but what about this wallpaper?
Or is it a kind of indoor cemetery?
There's something about death going on here.

In fact, I start to wonder if what we have here
is really two poems, or three, or four,
or possibly none.

But then there's that last stanza, my favorite.
This is where the poem wins me back,
especially the lines spoken in the voice of the mouse.
I mean we've all seen these images in cartoons before,
but I still love the details he uses
when he's describing where he lives.
The perfect little arch of an entrance in the baseboard,
the bed made out of a curled-back sardine can,
the spool of thread for a table.
I start thinking about how hard the mouse had to work
night after night collecting all these things
while the people in the house were fast asleep,
and that gives me a very strong feeling,
a very powerful sense of something.
But I don't know if anyone else was feeling that.
Maybe that was just me.
Maybe that's just the way I read it.

Budapest

My pen moves along the page
like the snout of a strange animal
shaped like a human arm
and dressed in the sleeve of a loose green sweater.

I watch it sniffing the paper ceaselessly,
intent as any forager that has nothing
on its mind but the grubs and insects
that will allow it to live another day.

It wants only to be here tomorrow,
dressed perhaps in the sleeve of a plaid shirt,
nose pressed against the page,
writing a few more dutiful lines

while I gaze out the window and imagine Budapest
or some other city where I have never been.

My Heart

It has a bronze covering inlaid with silver,
originally gilt;
the sides are decorated with openwork zoomorphic
panels depicting events in the history
of an unknown religion.
The convoluted top-piece shows a high
level of relief articulation
as do the interworked spirals at the edges.

It was presumably carried in the house-shaped
reliquary alongside it, an object of exceptional
ornament, one of the few such pieces extant.
The handle, worn smooth, indicates its use
in long-forgotten rituals, perhaps
of a sacrificial nature.

It is engirdled with an inventive example
of gold interlacing, no doubt of Celtic influence.
Previously thought to be a pre-Carolingian work,
it is now considered to be of more recent provenance,
probably the early 1940s.

The ball at the center, visible
through the interstices of the lead webbing
and the elaborate copper grillwork,
is composed possibly of jelly
or an early version of water,
certainly a liquid, remarkably suspended
within the intricate craftsmanship of its encasement.

Dancing Toward Bethlehem

If there is only enough time in the final
minutes of the twentieth century for one last dance
I would like to be dancing it slowly with you,

say, in the ballroom of a seaside hotel.
My palm would press into the small of your back
as the past hundred years collapsed into a pile
of mirrors or buttons or frivolous shoes,

just as the floor of the nineteenth century gave way
and disappeared in a red cloud of brick dust.
There will be no time to order another drink
or worry about what was never said,

not with the orchestra sliding into the sea
and all our attention devoted to humming
whatever it was they were playing.

The First Dream

The wind is ghosting around the house tonight,
and as I lean against the door of sleep
I begin to think about the first person to dream,
how quiet he must have seemed the next morning

as the others stood around the fire
draped in the skins of animals
talking to each other only in vowels,
for this was long before the invention of consonants.

He might have gone off by himself to sit
on a rock and look into the mist of a lake
as he tried to tell himself what had happened,
how he had gone somewhere without going,

how he had put his arms around the neck
of a beast that the others could touch
only after they had killed it with stones,
how he felt its breath on his bare neck.

Then again, the first dream could have come
to a woman, though she would behave,
I suppose, much the same way,
moving off by herself to be alone near water,

except that the curve of her young shoulders
and the tilt of her downcast head
would make her appear to be terribly alone,
and if you were there to notice this,

you might have gone down as the first person
to ever fall in love with the sadness of another.

Sweet Talk

You are not the Mona Lisa
with that relentless look.
Or Venus borne over the froth
of waves on a pink half shell.
Or an odalisque by Delacroix,
veils lapping at your nakedness.

You are more like the sunlight
of Edward Hopper,
especially when it slants
against the eastern side
of a white clapboard house
in the early hours of the morning,
with no figure standing
at a window in a violet bathrobe,
just the sunlight,
the columns of the front porch,
and the long shadows
they throw down
upon the dark green lawn, baby.

Man in Space

All you have to do is listen to the way a man
sometimes talks to his wife at a table of people
and notice how intent he is on making his point
even though her lower lip is beginning to quiver,

and you will know why the women in science
fiction movies who inhabit a planet of their own
are not pictured making a salad or reading a magazine
when the men from earth arrive in their rocket,

why they are always standing in a semicircle
with their arms folded, their bare legs set apart,
their breasts protected by hard metal disks.

Center

At the first chink of sunrise,
the windows on one side of the house
are frosted with stark orange light,

and in every pale blue window
on the other side
a full moon hangs, a round, white blaze.

I look out one side, then the other,
moving from room to room
as if between countries or parts of my life.

Then I stop and stand in the middle,
extend both arms
like Leonardo's man, naked in a perfect circle.

And when I begin to turn slowly
I can feel the whole house turning with me,
rotating free of the earth.

The sun and moon in all the windows
move, too, with the tips of my fingers,
the solar system turning by degrees

with me, morning's egomaniac,
turning on the hallway carpet in my slippers,
taking the cold orange, blue, and white

for a quiet, unhurried spin,
all wheel and compass, axis and reel,
as wide awake as I will ever be.

Design

I pour a coating of salt on the table
and make a circle in it with my finger.
This is the cycle of life
I say to no one.
This is the wheel of fortune,
the Arctic Circle.
This is the ring of Kerry
and the white rose of Tralee
I say to the ghosts of my family,
the dead fathers,
the aunt who drowned,
my unborn brothers and sisters,
my unborn children.
This is the sun with its glittering spokes
and the bitter moon.
This is the absolute circle of geometry
I say to the crack in the wall,
to the birds who cross the window.
This is the wheel I just invented
to roll through the rest of my life
I say
touching my finger to my tongue.

Piano Lessons

1

My teacher lies on the floor with a bad back
off to the side of the piano.
I sit up straight on the stool.
He begins by telling me that every key
is like a different room
and I am a blind man who must learn
to walk through all twelve of them
without hitting the furniture.
I feel myself reach for the first doorknob.

2

He tells me that every scale has a shape
and I have to learn how to hold
each one in my hands.
At home I practice with my eyes closed.
C is an open book.
D is a vase with two handles.
G flat is a black boot.
E has the legs of a bird.

3

He says the scale is the mother of the chords.
I can see her pacing the bedroom floor
waiting for her children to come home.
They are out at nightclubs shading and lighting
all the songs while couples dance slowly
or stare at one another across tables.
This is the way it must be. After all,
just the right chord can bring you to tears
but no one listens to the scales,
no one listens to their mother.

4

I am doing my scales,
the familiar anthems of childhood.
My fingers climb the ladder of notes
and come back down without turning around.
Anyone walking under this open window
would picture a girl of about ten
sitting at the keyboard with perfect posture,
not me slumped over in my bathrobe, disheveled,
like a white Horace Silver.

5

I am learning to play
'It Might As Well Be Spring'
but my left hand would rather be jingling
the change in the darkness of my pocket
or taking a nap on an armrest.
I have to drag him into the music
like a difficult and neglected child.
This is the revenge of the one who never gets
to hold the pen or wave good-bye,
and now, who never gets to play the melody.

6

Even when I am not playing, I think about the piano.
It is the largest, heaviest,
and most beautiful object in this house.
I pause in the doorway just to take it all in.
And late at night I picture it downstairs,
this hallucination standing on three legs,
this curious beast with its enormous moonlit smile.

The Blues

Much of what is said here
must be said twice,
a reminder that no one
takes an immediate interest in the pain of others.

Nobody will listen, it would seem,
if you simply admit
your baby left you early this morning
she didn't even stop to say good-bye.

But if you sing it again
with the help of the band
which will now lift you to a higher,
more ardent and beseeching key,

people will not only listen;
they will shift to the sympathetic
edges of their chairs,
moved to such acute anticipation

by that chord and the delay that follows,
they will not be able to sleep
unless you release with one finger
a scream from the throat of your guitar

and turn your head back to the microphone
to let them know
you're a hard-hearted man
but that woman's sure going to make you cry.

Nightclub

You are so beautiful and I am a fool
to be in love with you
is a theme that keeps coming up
in songs and poems.
There seems to be no room for variation.
I have never heard anyone sing
I am so beautiful
and you are a fool to be in love with me,
even though this notion has surely
crossed the minds of women and men alike.
You are so beautiful, too bad you are a fool
is another one you don't hear.
Or, you are a fool to consider me beautiful.
That one you will never hear, guaranteed.

For no particular reason this afternoon
I am listening to Johnny Hartman
whose dark voice can curl around
the concepts of love, beauty, and foolishness
like no one else's can.
It feels like smoke curling up from a cigarette
someone left burning on a baby grand piano
around three o'clock in the morning;

smoke that billows up into the bright lights
while out there in the darkness
some of the beautiful fools have gathered
around little tables to listen,
some with their eyes closed,
others leaning forward into the music
as if it were holding them up,
or twirling the loose ice in a glass,
slipping by degrees into a rhythmic dream.

Yes, there is all this foolish beauty,
borne beyond midnight,
that has no desire to go home,
especially now when everyone in the room
is watching the large man with the tenor sax
that hangs from his neck like a golden fish.
He moves forward to the edge of the stage
and hands the instrument down to me
and nods that I should play.
So I put the mouthpiece to my lips
and blow into it with all my living breath.
We are all so foolish,
my long bebop solo begins by saying,
so damn foolish
we have become beautiful without even knowing it.

Some Final Words

I cannot leave you without saying this:
the past is nothing,
a nonmemory, a phantom,
a soundproof closet in which Johann Strauss
is composing another waltz no one can hear.

It is a fabrication, best forgotten,
a wellspring of sorrow
that waters a field of bitter vegetation.

Leave it behind.
Take your head out of your hands
and arise from the couch of melancholy
where the window-light falls against your face
and the sun rides across the autumn sky,
steely behind the bare trees,
glorious as the high strains of violins.

But forget Strauss.
And forget his younger brother,
the poor bastard who was killed in a fall
from a podium while conducting a symphony.

Forget the past,
forget the stunned audience on its feet,
the absurdity of their formal clothes
in the face of sudden death,
forget their collective gasp,
the murmur and huddle over the body,
the creaking of the lowered curtain.

Forget Strauss
with that encore look in his eye
and his tiresome industry:
more than five hundred finished compositions!
He even wrote a polka for his mother.
That alone is enough to make me flee the past,
evacuate its temples,
and walk alone under the stars
down these dark paths strewn with acorns,
feeling nothing but the crisp October air,
the swing of my arms
and the rhythm of my stepping –
a man of the present who has forgotten
every composer, every great battle,
just me,
a thin reed blowing in the night.

from

Picnic, Lightning

Fishing on the Susquehanna in July

I have never been fishing on the Susquehanna
or on any river for that matter
to be perfectly honest.

Not in July or any month
have I had the pleasure – if it is a pleasure –
of fishing on the Susquehanna.

I am more likely to be found
in a quiet room like this one –
a painting of a woman on the wall,

a bowl of tangerines on the table –
trying to manufacture the sensation
of fishing on the Susquehanna.

There is little doubt
that others have been fishing
on the Susquehanna,

rowing upstream in a wooden boat,
sliding the oars under the water
then raising them to drip in the light.

But the nearest I have ever come to
fishing on the Susquehanna
was one afternoon in a museum in Philadelphia

when I balanced a little egg of time
in front of a painting
in which that river curled around a bend

under a blue cloud-ruffled sky,
dense trees along the banks,
and a fellow with a red bandanna

sitting in a small, green
flat-bottom boat
holding the thin whip of a pole.

That is something I am unlikely
ever to do, I remember
saying to myself and the person next to me.

Then I blinked and moved on
to other American scenes
of haystacks, water whitening over rocks,

even one of a brown hare
who seemed so wired with alertness
I imagined him springing right out of the frame.

To a Stranger Born in Some Distant Country Hundreds of Years from Now

'I write poems for a stranger who will be born in some
distant country hundreds of years from now.'

– Mary Oliver

Nobody here likes a wet dog.
No one wants anything to do with a dog
that is wet from being out in the rain
or retrieving a stick from a lake.
Look how she wanders around the crowded pub tonight
going from one person to another
hoping for a pat on the head, a rub behind the ears,
something that could be given with one hand
without even wrinkling the conversation.

But everyone pushes her away,
some with a knee, others with the sole of a boot.
Even the children, who don't realize she is wet
until they go to pet her,
push her away
then wipe their hands on their clothes.
And whenever she heads toward me,
I show her my palm, and she turns aside.

O stranger of the future!
O inconceivable being!
whatever the shape of your house,
however you scoot from place to place,
no matter how strange and colorless the clothes you may wear,
I bet nobody there likes a wet dog either.
I bet everybody in your pub,
even the children, pushes her away.

I Chop Some Parsley While Listening to Art Blakey's Version of 'Three Blind Mice'

And I start wondering how they came to be blind.
If it was congenital, they could be brothers and sisters,
and I think of the poor mother
brooding over her sightless young triplets.

Or was it a common accident, all three caught
in a searing explosion, a firework perhaps?
If not,
if each came to his or her blindness separately,

how did they ever manage to find one another?
Would it not be difficult for a blind mouse
to locate even one fellow mouse with vision
let alone two other blind ones?

And how, in their tiny darkness,
could they possibly have run after a farmer's wife
or anyone else's wife for that matter?
Not to mention why.

Just so she could cut off their tails
with a carving knife, is the cynic's answer,
but the thought of them without eyes
and now without tails to trail through the moist grass

or slip around the corner of a baseboard
has the cynic who always lounges within me
up off his couch and at the window
trying to hide the rising softness that he feels.

By now I am on to dicing an onion
which might account for the wet stinging
in my own eyes, though Freddie Hubbard's
mournful trumpet on 'Blue Moon,'

which happens to be the next cut,
cannot be said to be making matters any better.

Afternoon with Irish Cows

There were a few dozen who occupied the field
across the road from where we lived,
stepping all day from tuft to tuft,
their big heads down in the soft grass,
though I would sometimes pass a window
and look out to see the field suddenly empty
as if they had taken wing, flown off to another county.

Then later, I would open the blue front door,
and again the field would be full of their munching,
or they would be lying down
on the black and white maps of their sides,
facing in all directions, waiting for rain.
How mysterious, how patient and dumbfounded
they appeared in the long quiet of the afternoons.

But every once in a while, one of them
would let out a sound so phenomenal
that I would put down the paper
or the knife I was cutting an apple with
and walk across the road to the stone wall
to see which one of them was being torched
or pierced through the side with a long spear.

Yes, it sounded like pain until I could see
the noisy one, anchored there on all fours,
her neck outstretched, her bellowing head
laboring upward as she gave voice
to the rising, full-bodied cry
that began in the darkness of her belly
and echoed up through her bowed ribs into her gaping mouth.

Then I knew that she was only announcing
the large, unadulterated cowness of herself,
pouring out the ancient apologia of her kind
to all the green fields and the gray clouds,
to the limestone hills and the inlet of the blue bay,
while she regarded my head and shoulders
above the wall with one wild, shocking eye.

Marginalia

Sometimes the notes are ferocious,
skirmishes against the author
raging along the borders of every page
in tiny black script.
If I could just get my hands on you,
Kierkegaard, or Conor Cruise O'Brien,
they seem to say,
I would bolt the door and beat some logic into your head.

Other comments are more offhand, dismissive –
'Nonsense.' 'Please!' 'HA!!' –
that kind of thing.
I remember once looking up from my reading,
my thumb as a bookmark,
trying to imagine what the person must look like
who wrote, 'Don't be a ninny'
alongside a paragraph in *The Life of Emily Dickinson*.

Students are more modest
needing to leave only their splayed footprints
along the shore of the page.
One scrawls 'Metaphor' next to a stanza of Eliot's.
Another notes the presence of 'Irony'
fifty times outside the paragraphs of *A Modest Proposal*.

Or they are fans who cheer from the empty bleachers,
hands cupped around their mouths.
'Absolutely,' they shout
to Duns Scotus and James Baldwin.
'Yes.' 'Bull's-eye.' 'My man!'
Check marks, asterisks, and exclamation points
rain down along the sidelines.

And if you have managed to graduate from college
without ever having written 'Man vs. Nature'
in a margin, perhaps now
is the time to take one step forward.

We have all seized the white perimeter as our own
and reached for a pen if only to show
we did not just laze in an armchair turning pages;
we pressed a thought into the wayside,
planted an impression along the verge.

Even Irish monks in their cold scriptoria
jotted along the borders of the Gospels
brief asides about the pains of copying,
a bird singing near their window,
or the sunlight that illuminated their page –
anonymous men catching a ride into the future
on a vessel more lasting than themselves.

And you have not read Joshua Reynolds,
they say, until you have read him
enwreathed with Blake's furious scribbling.

Yet the one I think of most often,
the one that dangles from me like a locket,
was written in the copy of *Catcher in the Rye*
I borrowed from the local library
one slow, hot summer.
I was just beginning high school then,
reading books on a davenport in my parents' living room,
and I cannot tell you
how vastly my loneliness was deepened,
how poignant and amplified the world before me seemed,
when I found on one page

a few greasy looking smears
and next to them, written in soft pencil –
by a beautiful girl, I could tell,
whom I would never meet –
'Pardon the egg salad stains, but I'm in love.'

Some Days

Some days I put the people in their places at the table,
bend their legs at the knees,
if they come with that feature,
and fix them into the tiny wooden chairs.

All afternoon they face one another,
the man in the brown suit,
the woman in the blue dress,
perfectly motionless, perfectly behaved.

But other days, I am the one
who is lifted up by the ribs,
then lowered into the dining room of a dollhouse
to sit with the others at the long table.

Very funny,
but how would you like it
if you never knew from one day to the next
if you were going to spend it

striding around like a vivid god,
your shoulders in the clouds,
or sitting down there amidst the wallpaper,
staring straight ahead with your little plastic face?

Picnic, Lightning

'My very photogenic mother died in a freak accident
(picnic, lightning) when I was three.'

– Lolita

It is possible to be struck by a meteor
or a single-engine plane
while reading in a chair at home.
Safes drop from rooftops
and flatten the odd pedestrian
mostly within the panels of the comics,
but still, we know it is possible,
as well as the flash of summer lightning,
the thermos toppling over,
spilling out on the grass.

And we know the message
can be delivered from within.
The heart, no valentine,
decides to quit after lunch,
the power shut off like a switch,
or a tiny dark ship is unmoored
into the flow of the body's rivers,
the brain a monastery,
defenseless on the shore.

This is what I think about
when I shovel compost
into a wheelbarrow,
and when I fill the long flower boxes,
then press into rows
the limp roots of red impatiens –
the instant hand of Death
always ready to burst forth
from the sleeve of his voluminous cloak.

Then the soil is full of marvels,
bits of leaf like flakes off a fresco,
red-brown pine needles, a beetle quick
to burrow back under the loam.
Then the wheelbarrow is a wilder blue,
the clouds a brighter white,

and all I hear is the rasp of the steel edge
against a round stone,
the small plants singing
with lifted faces, and the click
of the sundial
as one hour sweeps into the next.

Morning

Why do we bother with the rest of the day,
the swale of the afternoon,
the sudden dip into evening,

then night with his notorious perfumes,
his many-pointed stars?

This is the best –
throwing off the light covers,
feet on the cold floor,
and buzzing around the house on espresso –

maybe a splash of water on the face,
a palmful of vitamins –
but mostly buzzing around the house on espresso,

dictionary and atlas open on the rug,
the typewriter waiting for the key of the head,
a cello on the radio,

and, if necessary, the windows –
trees fifty, a hundred years old
out there,
heavy clouds on the way
and the lawn steaming like a horse
in the early morning.

Bonsai

All it takes is one to throw a room
completely out of whack.

Over by the window
it looks hundreds of yards away,

a lone stark gesture of wood
on the distant cliff of a table.

Up close, it draws you in,
cuts everything down to its size.

Look at it from the doorway,
and the world dilates and bloats.

The button lying next to it
is now a pearl wheel,

the book of matches is a raft,
and the coffee cup a cistern

to catch the same rain
that moistens its small plot of dark, mossy earth.

For it even carries its own weather,
leaning away from a fierce wind

that somehow blows
through the calm tropics of this room.

The way it bends inland at the elbow
makes me want to inch my way

to the very top of its spiky greenery,
hold onto for dear life

and watch the sea storm rage,
hoping for a tiny whale to appear.

I want to see her plunging forward
through the troughs,

tunneling under the foam and spindrift
on her annual, thousand-mile journey.

Shoveling Snow with Buddha

In the usual iconography of the temple or the local Wok
you would never see him doing such a thing,
tossing the dry snow over the mountain
of his bare, round shoulder,
his hair tied in a knot,
a model of concentration.

Sitting is more his speed, if that is the word
for what he does, or does not do.

Even the season is wrong for him.
In all his manifestations, is it not warm and slightly humid?
Is this not implied by his serene expression,
that smile so wide it wraps itself around the waist of the
     universe?

But here we are, working our way down the driveway,
one shovelful at a time.
We toss the light powder into the clear air.
We feel the cold mist on our faces.
And with every heave we disappear
and become lost to each other
in these sudden clouds of our own making,
these fountain-bursts of snow.

This is so much better than a sermon in church,
I say out loud, but Buddha keeps on shoveling.
This is the true religion, the religion of snow,
and sunlight and winter geese barking in the sky,
I say, but he is too busy to hear me.

He has thrown himself into shoveling snow
as if it were the purpose of existence,
as if the sign of a perfect life were a clear driveway
you could back the car down easily
and drive off into the vanities of the world
with a broken heater fan and a song on the radio.

All morning long we work side by side,
me with my commentary
and he inside the generous pocket of his silence,
until the hour is nearly noon
and the snow is piled high all around us;
then, I hear him speak.

After this, he asks,
can we go inside and play cards?

Certainly, I reply, and I will heat some milk
and bring cups of hot chocolate to the table
while you shuffle the deck,
and our boots stand dripping by the door.

Aaah, says the Buddha, lifting his eyes
and leaning for a moment on his shovel
before he drives the thin blade again
deep into the glittering white snow.

Snow

I cannot help noticing how this slow Monk solo
seems to go somehow
with the snow
that is coming down this morning,

how the notes and the spaces accompany
its easy falling
on the geometry of the ground,
on the flagstone path,
the slanted roof,
and the angles of the split rail fence

as if he had imagined a winter scene
as he sat at the piano
late one night at the Five Spot
playing 'Ruby My Dear.'

Then again, it's the kind of song
that would go easily with rain
or a tumult of leaves,

and for that matter it's a snow
that could attend
an adagio for strings,
the best of the Ronettes,
or George Thorogood and the Destroyers.

It falls so indifferently
into the spacious white parlor of the world,
if I were sitting here reading
in silence,

reading the morning paper
or reading *Being and Nothingness*
not even letting the spoon
touch the inside of the cup,
I have a feeling
the snow would even go perfectly with that.

Japan

Today I pass the time reading
a favorite haiku,
saying the few words over and over.

It feels like eating
the same small, perfect grape
again and again.

I walk through the house reciting it
and leave its letters falling
through the air of every room.

I stand by the big silence of the piano and say it.
I say it in front of a painting of the sea.
I tap out its rhythm on an empty shelf.

I listen to myself saying it,
then I say it without listening,
then I hear it without saying it.

And when the dog looks up at me,
I kneel down on the floor
and whisper it into each of his long white ears.

It's the one about the one-ton
temple bell
with the moth sleeping on its surface,

and every time I say it, I feel the excruciating
pressure of the moth
on the surface of the iron bell.

When I say it at the window,
the bell is the world
and I am the moth resting there.

When I say it into the mirror,
I am the heavy bell
and the moth is life with its papery wings.

And later, when I say it to you in the dark,
you are the bell,
and I am the tongue of the bell, ringing you,

and the moth has flown
from its line
and moves like a hinge in the air above our bed.

Victoria's Secret

The one in the upper left-hand corner
is giving me a look
that says I know you are here
and I have nothing better to do
for the remainder of human time
than return your persistent but engaging stare.
She is wearing a deeply scalloped
flame-stitch halter top
with padded push-up styling
and easy side-zip tap pants.

The one on the facing page, however,
who looks at me over her bare shoulder,
cannot hide the shadow of annoyance in her brow.
You have interrupted me,
she seems to be saying,
with your coughing and your loud music.
Now please leave me alone;
let me finish whatever it was I was doing
in my organza-trimmed
whisperweight camisole with
keyhole closure and a point d'esprit mesh back.

I wet my thumb and flip the page.
Here, the one who happens to be reclining
in a satin and lace merry widow
with an inset lace-up front,

decorated underwire cups and bodice
with lace ruffles along the bottom
and hook-and-eye closure in the back,
is wearing a slightly contorted expression,
her head thrust back, mouth partially open,
a confusing mixture of pain and surprise
as if she had stepped on a tack
just as I was breaking down
her bedroom door with my shoulder.

Nor does the one directly beneath her
look particularly happy to see me.
She is arching one eyebrow slightly
as if to say, so what if I am wearing nothing
but this stretch panne velvet bodysuit
with a low sweetheart neckline
featuring molded cups and adjustable straps.
Do you have a problem with that?!

The one on the far right is easier to take,
her eyes half-closed
as if she were listening to a medley
of lullabies playing faintly on a music box.
Soon she will drop off to sleep,
her head nestled in the soft crook of her arm,
and later she will wake up in her
Spandex slip dress with the high side slit,
deep scoop neckline, elastic shirring,
and concealed back zip and vent.

But opposite her,
stretched out catlike on a couch
in the warm glow of a paneled library,
is one who wears a distinctly challenging expression,
her face tipped up, exposing
her long neck, her perfectly flared nostrils.
Go ahead, her expression tells me,
take off my satin charmeuse gown
with a sheer, jacquard bodice
decorated with a touch of shimmering Lurex.
Go ahead, fling it into the fireplace.
What do I care, her eyes say, we're all going to hell anyway.

I have other mail to open,
but I cannot help noticing her neighbor
whose eyes are downcast,
her head ever so demurely bowed to the side
as if she were the model who sat for Coreggio
when he painted 'The Madonna of St Jerome,'
only, it became so ungodly hot in Parma
that afternoon, she had to remove
the traditional blue robe
and pose there in his studio
in a beautifully shaped satin teddy
with an embossed V-front,
princess seaming to mold the bodice,
and puckered knit detail.

And occupying the whole facing page
is one who displays that expression
we have come to associate with photographic beauty.
Yes, she is pouting about something,
all lower lip and cheekbone.
Perhaps her ice cream has tumbled
out of its cone onto the parquet floor.
Perhaps she has been waiting all day
for a new sofa to be delivered,
waiting all day in a stretch lace hipster
with lattice edging, satin frog closures,
velvet scrollwork, cuffed ankles,
flare silhouette, and knotted shoulder straps
available in black, champagne, almond,
cinnabar, plum, bronze, mocha,
peach, ivory, caramel, blush, butter, rose, and periwinkle.
It is, of course, impossible to say,
impossible to know what she is thinking,
why her mouth is the shape of petulance.

But this is already too much.
Who has the time to linger on these delicate
lures, these once unmentionable things?
Life is rushing by like a mad, swollen river.
One minute roses are opening in the garden
and the next, snow is flying past my window.
Plus the phone is ringing.
The dog is whining at the door.
Rain is beating on the roof.
And as always there is a list of things I have to do

before the night descends, black and silky,
and the dark hours begin to hurtle by,
before the little doors of the body swing shut
and I ride to sleep, my closed eyes
still burning from all the glossy lights of day.

Lines Composed Over Three Thousand Miles from Tintern Abbey

I was here before, a long time ago,
and now I am here again
is an observation that occurs in poetry
as frequently as rain occurs in life.

The fellow may be gazing
over an English landscape,
hillsides dotted with sheep,
a row of tall trees topping the downs,

or he could be moping through the shadows
of a dark Bavarian forest,
a wedge of cheese and a volume of fairy tales
tucked into his rucksack.

But the feeling is always the same.
It was better the first time.
This time is not nearly as good.
I'm not feeling as chipper as I did back then.

Something is always missing –
swans, a glint on the surface of a lake,
some minor but essential touch.
Or the quality of things has diminished.

The sky was a deeper, more dimensional blue,
clouds were more cathedral-like,
and water rushed over rock
with greater effervescence.

From our chairs we have watched
the poor author in his waistcoat
as he recalls the dizzying icebergs of childhood
and mills around in a field of weeds.

We have heard the poets long dead
declaim their dying
from a promontory, a riverbank,
next to a haycock, within a copse.

We have listened to their dismay,
the kind that issues from poems
the way water issues forth from hoses,
the way the match always gives its little speech on fire.

And when we put down the book at last,
lean back, close our eyes,
stinging with print,
and slip in the bookmark of sleep,

we will be schooled enough to know
that when we wake up
a little before dinner
things will not be nearly as good as they once were.

Something will be missing
from this long, coffin-shaped room,
the walls and windows now
only two different shades of gray,

the glossy gardenia drooping
in its chipped terra-cotta pot.
And on the floor, shoes, socks,
the browning core of an apple.

Nothing will be as it was
a few hours ago, back in the glorious past
before our naps, back in that Golden Age
that drew to a close sometime shortly after lunch.

Paradelle for Susan

I remember the quick, nervous bird of your love.
I remember the quick, nervous bird of your love.
Always perched on the thinnest, highest branch.
Always perched on the thinnest, highest branch.
Thinnest love, remember the quick branch.
Always nervous, I perched on your highest bird the.

It is time for me to cross the mountain.
It is time for me to cross the mountain.
And find another shore to darken with my pain.
And find another shore to darken with my pain.
Another pain for me to darken the mountain.
And find the time, cross my shore, to with it is to.

The weather warm, the handwriting familiar.
The weather warm, the handwriting familiar.
Your letter flies from my hand into the waters below.
Your letter flies from my hand into the waters below.
The familiar waters below my warm hand.
Into handwriting your weather flies you letter the from the.

I always cross the highest letter, the thinnest bird.
Below the waters of my warm familiar pain,
Another hand to remember your handwriting.
The weather perched for me on the shore.
Quick, your nervous branch flew from love.
Darken the mountain, time and find was my into it was
   with to to.

NOTE: The paradelle is one of the more demanding French fixed forms, first appearing in the *langue d'oc* love poetry of the eleventh century. It is a poem of four six-line stanzas in which the first and second lines, as well as the third and fourth lines of the first three stanzas, must be identical. The fifth and sixth lines, which traditionally resolve these stanzas, must use *all* the words from the preceding lines and *only* those words. Similarly, the final stanza must use *every* word from *all* the preceding stanzas and *only* those words.

Lines Lost Among Trees

These are not the lines that came to me
while walking in the woods
with no pen
and nothing to write on anyway.

They are gone forever,
a handful of coins
dropped through the grate of memory,
along with the ingenious mnemonic

I devised to hold them in place –
all gone and forgotten
before I had returned to the clearing of lawn
in back of our quiet house

with its jars jammed with pens,
its notebooks and reams of blank paper,
its desk and soft lamp,
its table and the light from its windows.

So this is my elegy for them,
those six or eight exhalations,
the braided rope of the syntax,
the jazz of the timing,

and the little insight at the end
wagging like the short tail
of a perfectly obedient spaniel
sitting by the door.

This is my envoy to nothing
where I say Go, little poem –
not out into the world of strangers' eyes,
but off to some airy limbo,

home to lost epics,
unremembered names,
and fugitive dreams
such as the one I had last night,

which, like a fantastic city in pencil,
erased itself
in the bright morning air
just as I was waking up.

The Many Faces of Jazz

There's the one where you scrunch up
your features into a look of pained concentration,
every riff a new source of agony,

and there's the look of existential bemusement,
eyebrows lifted, chin upheld by a thumb,
maybe a swizzle stick oscillating in the free hand.

And, of course, for ballads,
you have the languorous droop,
her eyes half-closed, lips slightly parted,
the head lolling back, flower on a stem,
exposing plenty of turtleneck.

There's the everything-but-the-instrument look
on the fellow at the front table,
the one poised to mount the bandstand,
and the classic crazy-man-crazy face,
where the fixed grin joins the menacing stare,
especially suitable for long drum solos.

And let us not overlook the empathetic
grimace of the listener
who has somehow located the body
of cold rage dammed up behind the playing
and immersed himself deeply in it.

As far as my own jazz face goes –
and don't tell me you don't have one –
it hasn't changed that much
since its debut in 1957.
It's nothing special, easy enough to spot
in a corner of any club on any given night.
You know it – the reptilian squint,
lips pursed, jaw clenched tight,
and, most essential, the whole
head furiously, yet almost imperceptibly
nodding
in total and absolute agreement.

Taking Off Emily Dickinson's Clothes

First, her tippet made of tulle,
easily lifted off her shoulders and laid
on the back of a wooden chair.

And her bonnet,
the bow undone with a light forward pull.

Then the long white dress, a more
complicated matter with mother-of-pearl
buttons down the back,
so tiny and numerous that it takes forever
before my hands can part the fabric,
like a swimmer's dividing water,
and slip inside.

You will want to know
that she was standing
by an open window in an upstairs bedroom,
motionless, a little wide-eyed,
looking out at the orchard below,
the white dress puddled at her feet
on the wide-board, hardwood floor.

The complexity of women's undergarments
in nineteenth-century America
is not to be waved off,
and I proceeded like a polar explorer
through clips, clasps, and moorings,
catches, straps, and whalebone stays,
sailing toward the iceberg of her nakedness.

Later, I wrote in a notebook
it was like riding a swan into the night,
but, of course, I cannot tell you everything –
the way she closed her eyes to the orchard,
how her hair tumbled free of its pins,
how there were sudden dashes
whenever we spoke.

What I can tell you is
it was terribly quiet in Amherst
that Sabbath afternoon,
nothing but a carriage passing the house,
a fly buzzing in a windowpane.

So I could plainly hear her inhale
when I undid the very top
hook-and-eye fastener of her corset

and I could hear her sigh when finally it was unloosed,
the way some readers sigh when they realize
that Hope has feathers,
that reason is a plank,
that life is a loaded gun
that looks right at you with a yellow eye.

The Night House

Every day the body works in the fields of the world
mending a stone wall
or swinging a sickle through the tall grass –
the grass of civics, the grass of money –
and every night the body curls around itself
and listens for the soft bells of sleep.

But the heart is restless and rises
from the body in the middle of the night,
leaves the trapezoidal bedroom
with its thick, pictureless walls
to sit by herself at the kitchen table
and heat some milk in a pan.

And the mind gets up too, puts on a robe
and goes downstairs, lights a cigarette,
and opens a book on engineering.
Even the conscience awakens
and roams from room to room in the dark,
darting away from every mirror like a strange fish.

And the soul is up on the roof
in her nightdress, straddling the ridge,
singing a song about the wildness of the sea
until the first rip of pink appears in the sky.
Then, they all will return to the sleeping body
the way a flock of birds settles back into a tree,

The Death of the Hat

Once every man wore a hat.

In the ashen newsreels,
the avenues of cities
are broad rivers flowing with hats.

The ballparks swelled
with thousands of strawhats,
brims and bands,
rows of men smoking
and cheering in shirtsleeves.

Hats were the law.
They went without saying.
You noticed a man without a hat in a crowd.

You bought them from Adams or Dobbs
who branded your initials in gold
on the inside band.

Trolleys crisscrossed the city.
Steamships sailed in and out of the harbor.
Men with hats gathered on the docks.

There was a person to block your hat
and a hatcheck girl to mind it
while you had a drink
or ate a steak with peas and a baked potato.
In your office stood a hat rack.

resuming their daily colloquy,
talking to each other or themselves
even through the heat of the long afternoon
Which is why the body – that house of voice
sometimes puts down its metal tongs, its nee
to stare into the distance,

to listen to all its names being called
before bending again to its labor.

The day war was declared
everyone in the street was wearing a hat.
And they were wearing hats
when a ship loaded with men sank in the icy sea.

My father wore one to work every day
and returned home
carrying the evening paper,
the winter chill radiating from his overcoat.

But today we go bareheaded
into the winter streets,
stand hatless on frozen platforms.

Today the mailboxes on the roadside
and the spruce trees behind the house
wear cold white hats of snow.

Mice scurry from the stone walls at night
in their thin fur hats
to eat the birdseed that has spilled.

And now my father, after a life of work,
wears a hat of earth,
and on top of that,
a lighter one of cloud and sky – a hat of wind.

Passengers

At the gate, I sit in a row of blue seats
with the possible company of my death,
this sprawling miscellany of people –
carry-on bags and paperbacks –

that could be gathered in a flash
into a band of pilgrims on the last open road.
Not that I think
if our plane crumpled into a mountain

we would all ascend together,
holding hands like a ring of skydivers,
into a sudden gasp of brightness,
or that there would be some common place

for us to reunite to jubilize the moment,
some spaceless, pillarless Greece
where we could, at the count of three,
toss our ashes into the sunny air.

It's just that the way that man has his briefcase
so carefully arranged,
the way that girl is cooling her tea,
and the flow of the comb that woman

passes through her daughter's hair . . .
and when you consider the altitude,
the secret parts of the engines,
and all the hard water and the deep canyons below . . .

well, I just think it would be good if one of us
maybe stood up and said a few words,
or, so as not to involve the police,
at least quietly wrote something down.

Where I Live

The house sits at one end of a two-acre trapezoid.
There is a wide lawn, a long brick path,
rhododendrons, and large, heavy maples.

Behind the geometry of the nine rooms,
the woods run up a hillside;
and across the road in front

is a stream called the Plum Brook.
It must have flowed through an orchard
that no longer exists.

Tomorrow early, I will drive down
and talk to the stonecutter,
but today I am staying home,

standing at one window, then another,
or putting on a jacket
and wandering around outside

or sitting in a chair
watching the trees full of light-green buds
under the low hood of the sky.

This is the first good rain to fall
since my father was buried last week,
and even though he was very old,

I am amazed at how the small drops
stream down the panes of glass,
as usual,

gathering,
as they always have,
in pools on the ground.

Aristotle

This is the beginning.
Almost anything can happen.
This is where you find
the creation of light, a fish wriggling onto land,
the first word of *Paradise Lost* on an empty page.
Think of an egg, the letter A,
a woman ironing on a bare stage
as the heavy curtain rises.
This is the very beginning.
The first-person narrator introduces himself,
tells us about his lineage.
The mezzo-soprano stands in the wings.
Here the climbers are studying a map
or pulling on their long woolen socks.
This is early on, years before the Ark, dawn.
The profile of an animal is being smeared
on the wall of a cave,
and you have not yet learned to crawl.
This is the opening, the gambit,
a pawn moving forward an inch.
This is your first night with her,
your first night without her.
This is the first part
where the wheels begin to turn,
where the elevator begins its ascent,
before the doors lurch apart.

This is the middle.
Things have had time to get complicated,
messy, really. Nothing is simple anymore.
Cities have sprouted up along the rivers
teeming with people at cross-purposes –
a million schemes, a million wild looks.
Disappointment unshoulders his knapsack
here and pitches his ragged tent.
This is the sticky part where the plot congeals,
where the action suddenly reverses
or swerves off in an outrageous direction.
Here the narrator devotes a long paragraph
to why Miriam does not want Edward's child.
Someone hides a letter under a pillow.
Here the aria rises to a pitch,
a song of betrayal, salted with revenge.
And the climbing party is stuck on a ledge
halfway up the mountain.
This is the bridge, the painful modulation.
This is the thick of things.
So much is crowded into the middle –
the guitars of Spain, piles of ripe avocados,
Russian uniforms, noisy parties,
lakeside kisses, arguments heard through a wall –
too much to name, too much to think about.

And this is the end,
the car running out of road,
the river losing its name in an ocean,
the long nose of the photographed horse
touching the white electronic line.
This is the colophon, the last elephant in the parade,
the empty wheelchair,
and pigeons floating down in the evening.
Here the stage is littered with bodies,
the narrator leads the characters to their cells,
and the climbers are in their graves.
It is me hitting the period
and you closing the book.
It is Sylvia Plath in the kitchen
and St Clement with an anchor around his neck.
This is the final bit
thinning away to nothing.
This is the end, according to Aristotle,
what we have all been waiting for,
what everything comes down to,
the destination we cannot help imagining,
a streak of light in the sky,
a hat on a peg, and outside the cabin, falling leaves.